KU-008-825

JAMAICA
BABYLON
ON
A
THIN
WIRE

Adrian Boot
Michael Thomas

THAMES AND HUDSON
LONDON

To Lynne

OCT 1977

RETURN TO
CHORLEYWOOD
C'WOOD 2601

HERTFORDSHIRE
LIBRARY SERVICE
972·92
8427972

Photographs by Adrian Boot

Any copy of this book issued by the publisher as a
paperback is sold subject to the condition that it shall not
by way of trade or otherwise be lent, re-sold, hired out
or otherwise circulated without the publisher's prior
consent in any form of binding or cover other than that
in which it is published and without a similar condition
including these words being imposed on a subsequent
purchaser.

© 1976 Thames and Hudson Ltd, London

All rights reserved. No part of this publication may be
reproduced or transmitted in any form or by any means,
electronic or mechanical, including photocopy, recording
or any information storage and retrieval system, without
permission in writing from the publisher.

Filmset by Keyspools Ltd., Golborne, Lancashire
Printed in Great Britain at the Alden Press, Oxford

JAMAICA

BABYLON
ON
A
THIN
WIRE

2-9>

Babylon is on a wire
Babylon is on a wire
An' it's a delicate wire.
An' if JAH, JAH never come 'ere
An' if JAH, JAH never come 'ere
He see I when I pass and gone . . .

Johnny Walker

Walking down the road with the pistol in your waist,
Johnny you're too bad.
Walking down the road with the machete in your waist,
Johnny you're too bad.
Just a-robbing and a-stabbing, and a-looting and a-shooting,
You know you're too bad.
One of these days you may hear a voice say, come.
Where you gonna run to?
You're gonna run to the law for rest, where there will be no
                                        more run.

Slickers

Spots makes it fours all round. Ezekiah lays a four-deuce, Rupert polishes off his bottle of Dragon and lays a four-three. Spots hoists up on his elbow, his last domino held high above his head and about to smash the game, when artful little Isaac Churchill comes up with the three-deuce that makes it a key game, six straight and a clean sheet to him and Ezekiah. Spots snarls. Ezekiah's opening up another couple of Dragons with his teeth and Isaac keeps rubbing it in, crowing, going *Clean sheet! Clean sheet!*, and Ezekiah's laughing so hard his eyes are bulging like bloodshot pingpong balls and his adenoids are backing up and threatening to choke him — it's all too much for Spots to take. He gets hold of a Dragon bottle and smashes it on Isaac's head. These boys have been playing for a while so there are plenty of Red Stripe bottles and Dragon Stout bottles lying about, and quick as a flash the knives are out and Isaac's bleeding from the right eye and Rupert's lost an earlobe, someone knocks out the light and they're up and running in the dark . . . leaving Isaac groping in the doorway, down on his knees in the scattered dominoes and broken glass.

Dominoes, you might think, is a kid's game. But when you're down in the dirt in a backyard in shantytown, sitting around in the rising stench with nothing better to do than hang around all day getting in each other's way, and nothing better to look forward to than the next Bruce Lee movie or a re-run somewhere of *Kiss of Death*, then the toss of a coin can start a fight, and anything as fraught with dangerous competition as a simple game of dominoes can get quickly out of hand and turn into grievous bodily harm and malicious wounding. It's — the pressure.

There's a lot of deep menacing talk going around shantytown about the pressure. And not just down in the stench. Up past Half-Way Tree around the new supermarket piazzas, all over Kingston, and way up in the hills on the canefields and five-acre farms, whenever a bunch of Rastas and Rude Boys find themselves in somebody's backyard, taking it easy on a pound and a half of some of the smoothest and most narcotic ganja in the world, what's on their mind all the time these days is the pressure. And when some old fool fuses his synapses on too much white rum and Nutriment and goes out and buggers a five-year-old child, everybody round about has a certain amount of sympathy for him, because they know it's not his fault, it's just the pressure got too heavy for him and he couldn't take it any longer. The poor old boy couldn't help but lash out at the nearest living thing. Everybody's feeling it, and the pressure like some sinister infection keeps on rising with the murder rate. It plays on the paranoia of the merchant classes and the business community locked up in their hilltop villas, with an uneasy eye on the kitchen girl and the kitchen girl's yardboy with the machete. They've got an intercom system connecting them to their neighbours just in case. They're scared stiff, and they have good reason to be. Every night, somebody gets caught in the crossfire — and not just trigger-happy kamikaze kids down in shantytown either, but prominent taxpayers and friends (and enemies) of the Government, shot from ambush in full view of their wives and children and not necessarily robbed — till nobody can be sure what's going on any more and everybody dreads to think, whether or not there's some kind of diabolical terrorist campaign behind it, or some kind of Sino-Syrian business vendetta, or Machiavellian party policy to justify a suspension of civil liberties and the democratic process, or if it's just the first sporadic convulsions of the imminent apocalypse. There are all these people on the streets with sticking plaster on their eyebrows and bandages on their heads. Even the beggars are carrying crowbars.

The Government recently decided that any sequences from films on cinema or television that showed guns beings carried or fired by any save uniformed policemen or soldiers should automatically be excised.

Mr Oswald (Ossie) McDonald, Trade Administrator, has reported to the police that his life had been threatened by an anonymous caller.

He told the cops that the caller told his secretary that 'Mr McDonald is one of the men listed to be shot and it will be done soon.'

Babylon on a t'in wire, the Rastas say, and what they mean is the whole island, as it struggles to cope with post-colonial adolescence in a world going broke, is threatening to come apart at the seams. There were tanks in the streets of Kingston not so long ago, and a spot six o'clock curfew in Montego Bay, helicopters with searchlights straffing shantytown, paramilitary shock troops charging around the countryside shooting down the ganja planes, grim draconian legislation introduced indefinite detention without trial for anyone found carrying a gun. Wartime measures, these, like Northern Ireland's, where there's a war on. There's not supposed to be a war on in Jamaica.

'Soon-come,' says Spots, drawing himself up into his most ferocious posture, nostrils flared, eyes smouldering with righteous anger, like George Foreman putting the hex on Smokin' Joe — 'Revolution soon-come!' But soon-come is soon enough in Jamaica. Nobody's getting up first thing in the morning and mixing molotovs and sweating over the mimeograph. The revolution Spots has in mind has no such logic — it's a matter of haphazard slapstick violence.

What happens is a couple of Rude Boys like Spots and Rupert go and see a re-run of *Kiss of Death*, to check out the scene near the end where Richard Widmark pushes the old granny down the stairs in her wheelchair — and laughs. That's the part Spots loves, the way Widmark's lips fold back from his gums and he laughs. When the panic hit in the spring of '74, the Government banned *Kiss of Death* and cut all the gun-play out of the movies coming into Jamaica. And seeing that the only movies that pull a crowd in Jamaica are rank gore or Kung-fu movies, all those cheap black-backlash ghetto horrors that came out after *Shaft* and *Superfly*, when they cut the violence all that's left is all the daft filler scenes that don't make any sense at all.

Anyway, Spots and Rupert would go and see *Kiss of Death* and then they'd end up in somebody's yard pie-eyed on too much Red Stripe and ganja.

An 18-year-old youth was shot dead at his home in Rema Sunday night when a group of armed men invaded the building. Police report that Erris Henderson was at H-Building Trench Town, shortly after 7 o'clock when a gang of men armed with shotguns and revolvers entered the premises.

A man was shot dead yesterday by a policeman in a passing patrol car, while shooting at another policeman who had arrested him minutes earlier.

And one minute they're feeling not too bad at all, and then somebody says something *personal*, and somebody else takes it *personal*, and next thing the knives are out and somebody gets hurt because they're so wired up and frustrated with themselves they've got to take it out on somebody else and it doesn't matter who. The other day, an old man got shot on his doorstep and robbed of his lunch — a couple of sandwiches and a soursop in a brown paper bag. Old Dennis, the Maroon, up on his dasheen patch in the bush outside Moore Town, says the Devil's got into those boys down there. But Ridley, who's younger, in his twenties, and spent six months in a steelworks in Sheffield, says the Devil is only poorness.

They're Christian kids from the country, most of them, who hit shantytown with high hopes, and all they found were too many people living in oil drums and fruit-crates and one-room plywood outhouses, with nothing inside except a formica dinette and a glass cabinet for the family china and a radio blasting. West Kingston, literally, is a garbage dump. It used to be a fishing village outside town, and then the city started reclaiming the harbour and they turned it into a dump. Soon, the Israelites appeared— lost tribes of dirt-poor unemployed, homeless scavengers and vagrant Rastas, all washed up there in the rising stench. They built shacks and huts out of cardboard and plywood and rusty old iron, and the

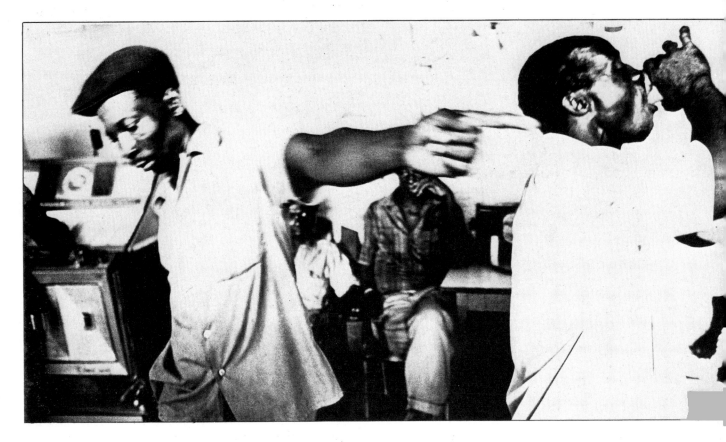

place spread like a disease till now it's teeming.
Kingston itself is in a basin, shut in by the Blue
Mountains, and in the summer, when the sun fries
the street and the asphalt begins to bubble and erupt
and the dirt and zinc-dust and nameless industrial
vapours hang in the air, down in Trench Town and
Jones Town and Tivoli Gardens and the other shantytowns down in West Kingston, you choke. In the
sixties the bulldozers moved in, the builders chased
the squatters off Ackee Walk and put up a few concrete highrises, but already they look like they're
ready to fall down and bury whole families alive.
West Kingston remains a bombsite landscape of live
garbage and boxwood and unlikely tropic greenery.

   And still they come to town, gangling teenage
runaways from the canefields and five-acre farms,
all looking for something faster than chopping cane
and humping bananas all their lives. Not sure, most
of them, what they're really looking for at all — except they all know about Jimmy Cliff and Desmond
Dekker and the rest of them, they were all just
country boys running with the Rude Boys until they
bluffed their way into Leslie Kong's record store or
somewhere with a little tune they'd written. They're
good, but every Rude Boy on Beeston Street reckons
he could do just as good as Jimmy Cliff, no trouble
at all, and Spots reckons he could probably do better,
he could make Jimmy beg.

   Just like they reckon if they could just get past
the residual colonial élitism of the selectors they
could give Lawrence Rowe 25 runs start and beat
him to 100, they could get in there first wicket down
and knock Thomson and Lillee from here to the
Gabba and back.

Errol Dixon, 19, who last month escaped from the St Catherine District Prison, was killed on Monday night in a confrontation with a police party in the shantytown area of Wareika Hills in Eastern Kingston.

According to the police, a party from Rock-fort station raided a yard in Wareika Hill where a dance was in session.

Dixon who was present, pulled a .303 rifle, said 'Police', and pointed it at a member of the party. He was immediately cut down by other policemen as he was about to pull the trigger.

Peter Wint, 18, labourer of Annotto Bay, was fatally shot on Monday night after he allegedly attacked the Police with a cutlass at Tanga Hill district in St Mary.

Mr Neville Bowes, 25, waiter and bartender, was slain by two gunmen on Friday night at his home in Kingston.

Police theory is that Mr Bowes was killed to prevent him from giving evidence in a murder case which is set for trial in the present session of the Home Circuit Court.

Mr Bowie was the chief witness in the case in which Mr John Camacho, divisional account-ant of Esso Standard Oil in Barbados, was fatally shot by gunmen on October 8 last at the Bamboo Club in Kingston.

Fifty-four-year-old Mr Ernest McDonald of Fourth Avenue, Kingston, was slain by gunmen, who robbed him of his lunch bag, shortly after he had left his home for work.

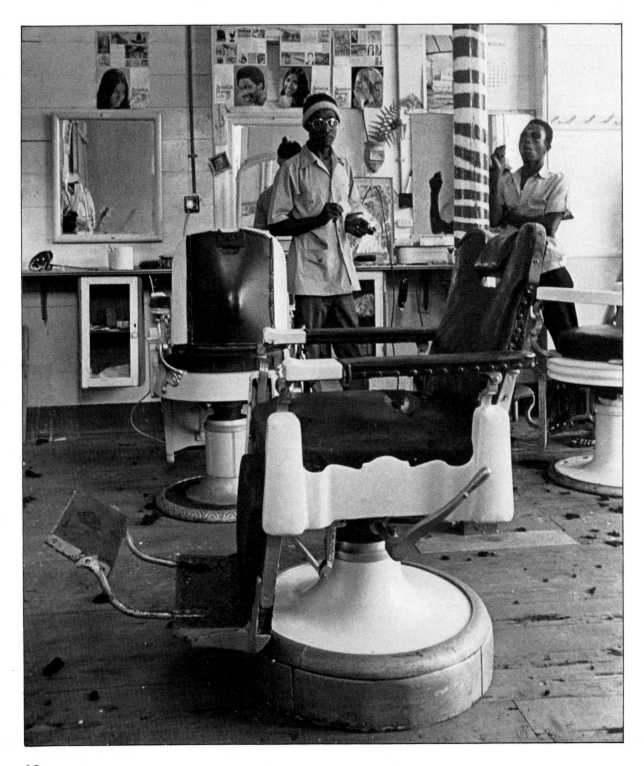

Bob's crew, took half an hour to get set up, but when they started just before 2.00 a.m. with the 'Rastafarian Chant', the audience realised that they were in for a treat.

Peter Tosh got the cops from Harman Barracks, moving out of the Stadium, with 'Mark of the Beast'. Bunny Livingstone played drums, and sang 'Arab Oil Weapon'.

Bob Marley was at home with the crowd of true fans who stayed behind singing all the tunes they requested.

Bob did 'Curfew', 'Bellyful', 'Knotty Dread', 'Trench Town Rock' and several more. Peter did '400 years' and two new songs including 'Legalise It'. When they ended, at about 3.45 a.m. the crowd brought them onstage again to do a couple more songs including 'Keep on Moving' and 'I Shot the Sherrif'.

The reason it was so simple for the shotgun producers like old Leslie Kong to burn the Rude Boys when the whole record business took off in the early sixties was because the Rude Boys didn't care. They'd never heard about royalties anyway, and they weren't going to sit still to be told. They were glad to grab ten dollars and get back down to shantytown and put themselves about — they were after the instant Karma. Then a kid like Jimmy Cliff could oh so casually take a pull on his bottle of Red Stripe at the Sound System and ask the brother next to him how he liked the sounds, and when the brother said it was a boss sound, Jimmy could roll his head back and close his eyes for a minute like the tune was really doing him in, and then snap out of it and say, oh so casually: 'That's I singin', y'know' — and crack a big horrible grin as the brother went green with envy.

That was the pie in the sky. Back in the thirties and forties, before Independence in 1962, Jamaican music was mostly just soundtrack for the swaying palms and silver sands and azure seas — bland and sleek and not too loud, just the speed for the swank resort lounges around Ocho Rios and Montego Bay. There were some suave Latin bands, and there was all that decaffeinated calypso. Calypso, in fact, is the singing journalism of Trinidad, polished, articulate stuff pitched halfway between insolence and insouciance. Jamaican calypso, what's called *mento*, is crude and simple, and back in the fifties the Baptists and the Church of God saw to it that the best *mento*, the lewd stuff, never got far out of the backyard. There was no record industry to speak of.

Down on the street, the kids were listening to the radio, to Fats Domino and Sam Cooke and the Coasters and the Drifters and all that low-rent ghetto rhythm and blues. They weren't allowed in anywhere, they didn't have any money, there was nowhere to go and nothing to do. So when some clever devil got hold of a couple of speakers and a pile of 45's and started running round all over West Kingston and up in the hills putting on backyard disco, Sound System caught on fast.

Soon there were a lot of them, and there still are, travelling deejays piling on more and more wattage and fighting over private stashes of hot 45's, each one trying to blitz out the other. Duke Reid used to arrive at his shows in flowing ermine, a mighty gold crown on his head, a Colt .45 in a cowboy holster, a shotgun over his shoulder and a cartridge belt slung across his chest. He was magnificent, gold rings on every finger and thumb, the dread double-image of Hollywood gangster and high camp aristocrat the Rude Boys go for. He'd have himself carried through the ruck to his turntables. And then he'd let one go, the latest Lloyd Price, a rare old Joe Turner, and while the record played, Duke would get on a mike and start deejaying, hollering 'Wake-it-up! Wake-it-up!' and 'Good God!' and 'Jump shake-a-leg!' and so on, just generally steaming up the atmosphere. It was war. Soon there were all these legendary operators like Duke and Prince Buster and Sir

in the early sixties, the record business took off. Pirated American pressings with the label scratched off so the competition wouldn't know who it was or where to get it passed hands for twenty dollars a copy. Prince Buster and Duke Reid were back and forth to America looking for scoops. But it was all going so fast, there just wasn't enough product. And around about that time, in the late fifties and early sixties, American pop went limp. So it wasn't long before the Sound System men started getting hold of a one-track or a two-track recorder and making their own records. It was easy. Duke was right there in his liquor store, Treasure Isle Liquors, in the thick of downtown Kingston. All the talent he needed was outside the betting shop across the street, hanging out all day with nothing to do.

The Sound System was still packing them in and still does, but the action switched to the record end, and anybody who could come up with the cash for some two-track time and get a record pressed was in business. The talent was lining up. There were Rude Boys and Rastas all over Kingston lining up looking for an opening, and nobody bothered about contracts or royalty statements or anything like that. The producer had it all his own way. He took the risk, he paid the deejays to get it on the radio, he took the credit and he got the money. It was wide-open. It was a lot like the rock and roll game in the ghettoes in the fifties.

It was called *ska*, then. Just a beat, a dead simple nagging upbeat that's so simple only illiterate Jamaicans can play it. The Rolling Stones and just about every other ranking outfit looking for a valve grind has been down at Dynamic Studios in Kingston, but they never get it right. Whatever it's been called, ska, bluebeat, rocksteady, or reggae, Jamaican beat is deceptive, there's more to it than you hear. It's clammy, pelvic, and it throbs like a headache, what old Randy down at Randy's Record Store in Kingston calls gummy, so gummy you could throw it up against a wall and it would stick. It works on the marrow and the membrane.

Coxsone and a lot of one-nighters all called King or Count or Pope or something grand like that, all piling on the wattage and voltage till the bass was so powerful you could hear it underwater and they had about as much sheer reverb as the human body can stand without backing up and going out of joint. Then it came down to who had the hottest playlist. In there, when the whole Sound System war peaked

In an incident late yesterday three men opened fire at a police patrol party in the Bumper Hall area off Spanish Town Road.

The police returned the fire. In the ensuing gunbattle which came to a climax in the May Pen cemetery, one man was shot dead and another held. The police recovered a .38 revolver and ammunition from the men.

It takes a while to penetrate the patois, and it's only lately that Bob Marley and the Wailers and Toots and the Maytals have got out of the back-yard, but now that reggae has cracked the big charts in America, the record business in Kingston is booming. It's like Nashville down there. Dynamic Sounds started off in a shed and these days its a vast complex of sixteen-track studios and pressing plants and office space, an autonomous economic republic surrounded by barbed wire and patrolled by armed guards to keep out the hopefuls who still show up every day and climb the walls — looking for an opening.

Bob Marley has got himself a BMW. And when somebody has the cheek to ask, how come a shanty-town Rasta like him is driving round in a big expensive car like that, he's ready for them — BMW, he says, that car meant for him — that BMW stands for Bob Marley and the Wailers.

What they used to do a few years ago, when there were still trams lurching around downtown Kingston at forty and fifty miles an hour, the mad dogs like Spots and Rupert used to play a kind of chicken where they'd wait for a number-nine-tram — that's with the number nine in the speed regulator which meant the driver was drunk with power and in the spirit of the thing and the tram was wound up and going as fast as it could, much too fast, in danger any minute of coming off the rails — and they'd leap on and off at high speed. Tram-hopping it was called. Sometimes they'd hop off one tram on to another one coming the other way, or else there was another manoeuvre where they'd hop on and off and then back on again, just catching the last bar. There was a character called Peter Lorre who won a lot of bets catching the last bar backwards — and he was so deadly cool he held a white rabbit in his arms the whole time. If you missed at forty miles an hour, you'd hit the street and break every bone in your body. A lot of tram-hoppers got mangled pretty badly, quite a few died on impact. That's what made it such a good sport.

Fourteen year old Leon Pennant of St Margaret's Bay in Portland, was found dead atop of the Kingston—Port Antonio train when it reached St Margaret's Bay on Wednesday evening. Police investigating the boy's death believe he hopped the train as it pulled out of Buff Bay and was crushed at a viaduct as the train proceeded on the way to St Margaret's Bay.

These days, now that the trams are gone, the kids go sky-diving on the trains. They get on top of the carriages and gamble on their balance when the train goes down a hill, arms outstretched and legs wide, testing themselves against the updraught, waiting until the last possible second before they duck the overhead viaducts, and then a split second longer, and then — instant Karma.

To prove who can run faster or jump higher or fuck longer or smoke more dope or argue a fine point of natural history with more diabolical cunning, and bombast — to stretch your cool and never crack, to the point where you can stop traffic with the sheer authority of your image and kill flies with the ferocity of your concentrated gaze — to be the coolest and deadliest and most debonair Johnny Too Bad on Beeston Street — that's the day-to-day showdown the Rude Boys live for. That's how they work off the pressure.

They can't get a job unless it's digging ditches, and they're too smart for that. They're too busy thieving and hustling and maybe looking for an opening in the wholesale ganja business, so they can get themselves an S-90, or even a CB-200. Now and then they catch a ride over the mountains to Montego Bay and move a little ganja to the American kids, crush up some Phensic and tell them it's cocaine, perhaps link up with some cockstruck neurotic from New York and take her breath away.

On race days they end up outside the betting shop. Across the street massive battered speakers outside the New York Record Mart will be pumping out the stuff — the reggae, Big Youth and the Heptones and the Wailers and the Maytals and Desmond Dekker, a new one by Burning Spear. And if they've got a horse running out at Caymanas Park and George Ho Sang comes off the bend with a late run, they ride the beast all the way home, snapping their fingers. Not just a quick little snap, but a vicious whipping crack that takes perfect timing and long loose joints and bony knuckles, so that the fingers hit with the sharp crack of bone splintering . . .

Just the sort of deft digital flourish you need to whip out the blade of a ratchet knife — which is a particular kind of nicely curved blade in a tapered handle, made in Germany for gutting fish. It's a very well-made instrument, dirt cheap at a dollar fifty, and every kid is a master of knife play. They can really perform with a knife. They get their finger in the ring at the end of the handle and snap out the blade so fast it reminds you of that old World War II joke about the Ghurkas — when the German soldier comes face to face with a Ghurka, and the Ghurka whips out his sword and swipes and seems to miss. 'Missed,' says the German. 'Shake your head,' says the Ghurka.

Well, the Rude Boys are faster than that. They make Ghurkas look spastic. They can snap out the blade faster than you can gasp for breath, just to oh so nonchalantly pick a seed out of their teeth or slice off a bothersome hangnail.

Machetes are cheap too — two and half feet of Sheffield steel goes for less than two dollars. And these are country boys, most of them — if they're not fresh off the canefields their fathers were, and up in the country nobody goes anywhere without his machete in his belt, or dangling from his fingertips, slapping his leg. Just in case he gets in the mood to clear his dasheen patch, or chop down a couple of coconuts, or just hack away at the nearest tree trunk for no real reason at all, to exercise his arm, perhaps, or test his edge, more often because something comes over him, some sudden incoherent unease, and he feels the need to make his presence felt.

Leroy Sinclair, 18, of Buff Bay in Portland, was on Thursday found guilty of illegal possession of six rounds of ammunition, and sentenced to three years imprisonment.

Sinclair made history of a sort, for being the first man to be convicted in the Gun Court.

Under the Gun Court Act, which came into force on April 1, the sentence for anyone found guilty of an offence under the Act is indefinite detention. However, Sinclair committed his offence before the act was enforced.

Paul Hudson, alias 'Rat Ears', 17-year-old labourer, was sentenced to indefinite detention by Resident Magistrate Mr E. G. Green in the Gun Court yesterday.

Hudson was charged with illegal possession of a firearm and was represented by Mr Richard Small.

During the hearing, the Magistrate directed that no details of the case be published because there were other charges pending against the accused as a result of the same incident.

An appeal to all citizens of goodwill to help destroy the guns

Take the guns to church.

If you have illegal guns in your possession or know of any —
you're invited by the Minister of National Security and Justice to:-
    leave them in any church hall
    hand them to any Minister of Religion.

Look for the guns.

Search all empty lots and gully courses to locate firearms that have been discarded.
Then phone 119, or report to your nearest police station.
The police will do the rest.

THE GUN COURT ACT STARTS TODAY   THE PENALTY IS INDEFINITE DETENTION

In the daily papers, these days, when the pressure gets too much for some poor fiend and he goes berserk and starts hacking up Violet and Sylvia in their beds, they tend to refer to his machete as a *cutlass*. Which strikes a flamboyant note, recalling the fabulous anarchy of Jamaica's pirate past, when the scourge of the Caribbean operated from Port Royal across Kingston Bay, and the scurviest and most barbarous of them all, Henry Morgan, was knighted by Charles II and made Lieutenant-Governor of the island.

The guns come into the island in different ways. One scandalous story that won't go away insists a lot of them arrived packed into refrigerators during the late sixties and were passed out wholesale by over-eager M P's campaigning in the hills. There is no way of knowing if that's true — there are few facts in Jamaica, only passionate partisan opinions. But there was a case not long ago where a PNP appointee and close acquaintance of Prime Minister Manley got shot. Somebody just walked up to him and shot him point blank. Manley led a state funeral procession through the streets which somehow took a wrong turn and found itself in rival JLP territory, and six mourners got shot from a speeding car.

You don't hear about it in England. The Jamaicans jammed into some airless basement in Brixton hear about it, but all you ever see in *The Times* or the overseas edition of the *Gleaner* are long, reasoned pieces about social relocation programmes trying to find some fruitful outlet for all that youthful energy going bad, like digging ditches on the road to May Pen or sweeping the Spanish Town road. West Kingston is under the gun, the streets are a battlefield, the Prime Minister gets shot at in the streets by hired political hit-men, and you never see a word.

They say most of the hand guns — and there are a hell of a lot of them — come in from America in exchange for ganja. Light planes from Florida land in the fields up in the hills, load up with tons of bulging crocus sacks and leave sawn-off shotguns

Three bullets were given as collection by an unknown man or his agent sometime during a religious service last Sunday at the Jones Town Salvation Army Hall. That's taking your ammo to church.

The Gun Court Act came into effect yesterday and quite a number of guns and ammunition were handed into churches in response to a final warning from the Minister of National Security and Justice, Mr Eli Matalon, to 'turn in your guns. Take your guns to the church.'

"Under the Gun Court Act, INDEFINITE DETENTION means, continuous imprisonment & loss of freedom" and Colt .45s as part of the deal. That's the official version, but nobody believes that either. All the Too Bad Boys have got a gun, or they can get hold of one as easily as hitting an old man on the head. That makes you a dread man, if you've got a gun. Like Spots' friend Silver Dollar. He just goes by the name Silver Dollar. He goes hauling by, double-declutching down into a 90 degree bend at 65 in his plum-coloured Cortina, which isn't exactly a 30-foot El Dorado with patent leather tyres and Texas longhorns for handles like you see on Seventh Avenue in New York, but he's got tigerfur seat-covers and they cost something. At least it's a car, and any black man with a car's doing all right. 'Him a dread man,' says Spots, as he disappears in a four-wheel drift, sending an approaching schoolbus that's doing about 40 in third itself on four bald tyres up on to the verge. 'That Silver Dollar,' says Spots, 'him a dread man. Him got a gun, y'know.' *Dread* means a lot. Dread is a word they use in Jamaica when no other word will do, meaning all that is deep and menacing and a threat to body and soul.

The murder rate hit epidemic in the spring of '74. So many people were getting shot each day the papers couldn't keep up, and then within a week three big names in the business community got shot. The Government shook with rage. Up in the hilltop villas the middle classes started calling Pan Am and getting together on the patio with their neighbours to try and figure out who was next. Manley's Defence Minister, Eli Matalon, threw up barbed-wire compounds like cattle corrals squat in the middle of Kingston. They painted them red because Manley said 'Red is dread.' He said he didn't like having to go to such lengths, and he hoped everyone would see reason and take their guns to church before the amnesty ended and let the Gun Courts stay empty and rust away. Parsons started getting ammunition clips in their collection bowls, kids found sawn-off shotguns thrown away in the grass. But down in the stench, where the guns are, the pressure backfired. The tanks moved in, and the police charged around busting people on the handy charge of being a suspicious person. The Gun Courts filled up fast, and when the Privy Council finally ruled indefinite detention unconstitutional, Manley did not let that stop him, he made it a mandatory life sentence without appeal. While he was about it, Matalon's successor came up with a new law — what's known as the utterance law, which makes any utterance construed as derogatory or intending to undermine constitutional authority an offence, and bars the felon from ever holding electoral office. Manley said you have to understand the legislation as part of a total philosophy in relation to crime and punishment.

There are so many convicted murderers awaiting execution on death row there's a waiting list, and Friday the hangman quit. And all it means is that the pressure is coming down heavier on the Too Bad Boys on the street already on the point of running amuck, and it makes them all the more determined to live fast, die young, and have a good looking corpse.

Four hundred years, an' it's the same, the same philosophy.
I've said it's four hundred years long, how long
And the people they still can't see.

Why do they fight against the poor youth of today.
If we love these youths they be
All gone astray.
Make a move. I can see the time has come
And if fools don't see . . .
I can't say if the youth, the youth is gonna be strong.
So won't you come with me,
I'll take you to a land of liberty,
Where we can live, live a good life
And be free.

Bob Marley

Noel Coward is buried on a hilltop overlooking Port Maria. He died there in his house, Blue Harbour, a few years ago.

Coward was one of the last of the sunstruck Caribbean voluptuaries, secure in his private stretch of paradise, high above the view. He'd lived there on and off since the late forties, not far from Ian Fleming at Oracabessa. Errol Flynn's place was further along the coast, outside Port Antonio — they turned it into a hotel, but it burnt down a few years ago and there's nothing much left.

Since Independence in 1962, Jamaica is no place for the world-weary and the idle rich. The polo classes have all gone. Those few who remain, too old or too stubborn or too touched by the midday sun to go home to Eastbourne, sleep with a gun by the door and talk longingly of the past, when Jamaica was a sultry tropic paradise, the great plantations flourished, and the black-folks chopped cane and humped bananas and sang songs.

The great plantations, in fact, haven't flourished for a long time. Not since way back in the 1800s when Wilberforce outlawed the slave trade. Emancipation came later, in the 1830s. The canefields went broke, the Great Houses were abandoned to the undergrowth, and the planters took one last look and shipped out before they got their throats cut. What followed were the droughts and famines of the mid-nineteenth century, raging cholera and smallpox, all met by such withering indifference on the part of the Government that the pressure finally peaked in Morant Bay on the South Coast in 1865, and the dirt poor and disaffected sacked the town, burnt down the Court House and murdered the ranking white population. They were led by a man called Paul Bogle of Stoney Gut.

The plantation Great Houses, those few still standing, have been vamped up and turned into luxury hotels in the hills above Montego Bay. Nearly ten per cent of the islands' working population is still

bent double chopping cane, but sugar has long ceased to be a lucrative enterprise, and despite inflated prices and favourable quotas, the industry is stricken by high production costs and perilously low profits, and the British companies are reluctant to reinvest in mechanization. The big outfits like Tate & Lyle only continue to prosper today because the chronic unemployment on the island guarantees an embarrassment of cheap labour — not slaves exactly, but the next best thing. The plantation owners — and for some reason, many of them are Scots — still live in the big houses high on top of the hill. The white plantation staff, the overseers and production mana-gers and so on, live in bungalows about half way down. And at the bottom, in a mean straggle of box-wood and corrugated iron, that's where the field workers live. The reason the planters have always lived on top of the hill is not simply for the marvellous godlike omniscience, though — it's the mosquitoes. Mosquitoes used to torment Jamaica. They never seemed to bother the slaves so much — the way flies don't bother livestock, it was said — but up on top of the hill, sitting around miles from their nearest neighbour and light-years from Piccadilly, the planters were driven mad by the loneliness and the heat and the slow torture of the mosquitoes.

They're not so bad now. The British sprayed the island about fifty years ago. They got rid of the mosquito, but what nobody knew, and still nobody can actually prove, was that the mosquito was the natural enemy of a mysterious insect vector that attacks the tops of palm trees. So that now, all along the coast, there are these weird landscapes, a panorama of headless palm trees, the very swaying palms of paradise standing there bereft, like lost telegraph poles.

It's a small island, about four and a half thousand square miles, with too many people, about two and a half million, and more than half of them in Kingston. And it's an island of immigrants. The last of the native Arawaks were wiped out by the Spanish more than four hundred years ago. When the British evicted the Spanish in the mid-seventeenth century, the slave trade was already thriving, and over the next hundred years it flourished into a mass migration. Bold young sea dogs left Liverpool every week for the Gold Coast, and made the Atlantic crossing with their holds packed to the rafters, on the simple arithmetic that the more of the poor brutes they started out with, the more they might deliver, if not in good health, at least able to stand. If they hit bad weather and lost a few days and water ran low, they simply threw a few over the side. A few squeamish Methodists like Wilberforce appealing to the conscience of the British people might say what they liked, Pitt could rhapsodize about the great African civilization of the future, but the slave captains and the planters knew better. The way they looked at it, they were dealing in livestock — these weren't human beings, they were brute savages, and you had to break their savage wills, the same way you would a horse's, for its own good. That meant you had to chain them up and flog them when they answered back, and if they answered back again you had to kill them in case the rest of them got ideas.

At the height of the trade as many as eighty-five ships a year left Liverpool — carrying ridiculous gifts to flatter the King of Dahomey. The British didn't actually go hunting in the jungles themselves, they

53

relied on the King and the other African slavers to ransack the villages of their more docile neighbours up-river. And there were never enough. The bigger and more prosperous the West Indies plantations became, the more slaves they needed, and the richer everyone got. The King of Dahomey got so fat on the proceeds he had an entire house and contents imported from Liverpool, and he slept in a four poster bed.

It was the biggest forced migration in the history of the world. In all thirty million slaves left Africa for the Americas. Fifteen million arrived. Those that reached Jamaica, those that didn't die of flux or fever or some mysterious paralysis of the will to live, were sold by scramble on the docks. Which meant they were herded into a corral for inspection, and whoever had the cash just charged into the ruck and grabbed whoever he like the look of. Quite often, of course, the competition would get out of hand, and there'd be a terrible struggle, with a drunken clergy- man on one arm and a planter's agent on the other, both tugging at the poor brute for all they were worth.

When the whole grisly business was finally abolished, the plantations languished until the British opened up a new route and started shipping in Chinese and Indians as indentured labour.

Today, Jamaica is a black African society with a Sino-Syrian mercantile élite, and a whiter-shade-of-tan middle-class minority still inhibited by the pre- tensions of a white colonial plantocracy that doesn't even live there any more. The whole fiction of Jamai- can nationality is in dispute. 'Out of many, one people' is the national motto. The trouble is, ninety per cent of the population is black and ninety per cent is poor, and they are the same people.

Up in the hills, in Moore Town and Maroon Town, the Maroons hang on to a tribal autonomy they never lost. They are descendents of the ones that got away — the slaves abandoned in haste by the Spanish when they fled to Cuba, and runaway Corra- mantees. The Corramantees were a particularly fero- cious tribe never widely enslaved in Africa, and once they got to Jamaica they were the first to run to the hills. Those that were caught were hung from trees till they rotted. But those that fled right into the interior ranges were never caught, and though the British sent the cavalry after them — and when the cavalry couldn't get a foot-hold, entire regiments of sweating redcoats, dragging massive cannons up into the mountains to bombard them into oblivion — the Maroons never surrendered, and never have. To this day they live in surly isolation up in the Cockpit Country. They answer not to Kingston but to their own Lieutenant-Colonel.

Down in the stench, the Rastafarians have defected altogether into an outcast astral Ethiopianism. On the street, the young black Jamaicans, stranded somewhere between self-hate and swank-ing arrogance, with no future that they can see in the rudderless mobility of Caribbean capital growth, are growing dread locks and defecting in droves. Just about everybody in Jamaica, the black kids who can't get rid of the idea they'd be better off in a betting shop in Brixton, the Syrians and the Chinese, the Rastas homesick for Ethiopia — they all spend at least half the time wishing they were somewhere else.

Since 1962, when a referendum voted to disestablish the foundering West Indian Federation and seize full independence, Jamaicans have been struggling to make the psychic aboutface that has baffled most of the post-colonial Third World. Obliged for more than four hundred years to be accustomed to a posture and a psychology of *dependence*, they have

been abruptly left to run their own affairs and settle their own disputes, and they are still in the plaguey grip of post-colonial trauma.

In the old days a bright boy who'd been to school and aspired to rank and respect in the community could fight for a place in the civil service or police force — that was about as high as he could climb. Since Independence, the bright and ambitious boys go into business or politics. The civil service has lost all its colonial swagger, has become demoralized, slothful, inert.

If you come home and find some clever devil's been in and thieved your watch again, and you go down to the police station in the morning, chances are you'll disturb the two constables on duty at breakfast. Which is white rum and Nutriment and a tight game of dominoes. And the first one will insist it's the second one's turn to investigate the crime, and the second one will be that much more adamant that on the contrary, he investigated last time, which the first one will more vehemently deny, until the whole thing goes back and forth a few more times

and by now they are both on their feet and ready to do each other actual bodily harm. Neither man will budge on principle and give the other the satisfaction of making a *boy* of him. In the end, they ring up a third constable and send him on the case. But the 'phone doesn't work. And when they get in the car to go and fetch him, they're out of gas and there's a queue a mile long at the nearest station. Somebody just jumped the queue, a punch is thrown, Spots grabs his ratchet knife . . .

Not long ago they had a bank surrounded, out near Anotto Bay, with a couple of gunmen holed up inside. The gunmen wouldn't answer their demands for surrender, so pretty soon the police got sick of waiting and went in shooting. They went in on two fronts, shooting anything that moved. When the shooting stopped, they found the gunmen had somehow vanished in the excitement and six policemen were dead or dying. With a transient underworld of dirt poor and disaffected to give the gunmen easy camouflage, the police haven't got a hope. When they do catch them — and they do because the

gunmen are just as rash and can't help pushing their luck until it runs out — when they do get the bastards into gaol, somehow they get hold of a hacksaw and escape.

The law operates erratically, in sudden vengeful spasms. Now and then, the Government and the *Gleaner* correspondents manage to get some pious Protestant umbrage going, and the police galvanize themselves and rush out and bust a handful of street punks and harmless Rastas. They burn the few ganja fields they can ever find, and on occasion they get closer to the heavy traffic and actually ambush a light plane loading up. But ganja is the one high-yield cash crop, and up in the hills all the five acre farmers with a dasheen patch and a few bananas, and if they're men of substance perhaps a couple of goats — they've all got ganja fields a day's walk over the next ridge, and often a field big enough for a light plane. And the heavy traffic is in the hands of a few unseen, unimpeachable wholesalers. There's so much money in it, it's estimated ganja is second only to bauxite as a source of cash revenue for the island.

Soldiers of the Jamaica Defence Force yesterday morning shot down a United States registered airplane at Braco in Trelawny, injuring the pilot and his woman passenger.

The plane which exploded and was completely destroyed by fire, was fired on after the pilot ignored a command halt and attempted to take off shortly after making a landing at the airstrip.

A midnight ambush, a shoot-out involving a machine-gun and a sea chase yesterday morning left the police with half a million dollars worth of ganja, firearms, a motor vessel and three motor vehicles.

57

It came as a considerable surprise to the record crowd which turned out to see the Nigerians play Jamaica that Black men played polo, and that it was not a game confined to White Imperialists.

Jamaica is hung both ways. As much as pride demands they free themselves from the habits and attitudes of four hundred years of dependence, their economic future is more and more dependent on overseas, and mostly American, investment. At the mercy of all that expensive pink flesh squeezed like blancmange into atrocious leisurewear, getting tanked on banana daiquiris while the local kids dive for pennies. Continental Hyatt House and Holiday Inn are in Montego Bay, and almost all the $100-a-day hotels along the North coast are American owned. And so is the bauxite.

The bauxite is the main vein of the economy. Alcoa and Alcan and the other big American and Canadian companies are gouging great red holes out of the interior at a few cents a ton to feed the smelters in America — and the smelting is where the profit comes in. Jamaica can't afford to run a smelter because it could never generate enough power. They'd have to dam the Rio Grand, and that's a popular day trip, rafting on the Rio Grand. Besides, there's a lot of country people who live up there who think it wouldn't be wise to disturb the spirits of the drowned. If you stare too long into its waters, they say, if you dare to swim in the Rio Grand without the protection of somebody local, the river will drag you under. Not the treacherous currents, but the spirits of the drowned will embrace you and drag you down into the fathomless murk.

The bauxite is precious stuff. There's not a lot of accessible bauxite in the world, and the ore is worth more to the Jamaican Gross National Product than tourism or anything else — especially now the word's out, and even the tourists secure in the leisure compounds of the North coast are feeling the fall-out, catching those sullen looks, seeing all those people covered in sticking-plaster and bandages, starting to feel the pressure and maybe not coming back next year. Bauxite's the red ore from which you extract aluminium and it could secure Jamaica a place in the junta of post-colonial nations suddenly holding industrial capital to ransom, because they've got the oil, the copper, whatever — the raw material. But they are selling the bauxite cheap. Manley's Government have been agitating for a bigger stake in the industry, or at least the right to see the figures. But Jamaica's black cabinet, though they have the power, and Manley has the evangelical political vision of a Caribbean Wedgewood Benn, they lack the confidence in their own expertise and they have grave

In England...
they pay a lot for this
...but nothing for this
Take care of the banana
It's up to you what they pay

doubts about the enthusiasm of their workforce, so they don't insist too much for fear they would imperil the existing understanding and be left to mine the stuff themselves. Jamaica gets a hefty royalty for the bauxite. And the big companies keep casually mentioning that they should count their blessings because they could always get the stuff somewhere else if it stopped being worth their while, which probably isn't true. Too many of policy decisions affecting the Jamaican economy are made in New York and Toronto, the management and technical expertise in the field are American, and the profits are presumably so embarrassing that they have thought it best not to disclose them for fear the shock might bury them. Only the labour is Jamaican. They do the digging.

The bauxite business, like the banana business, and the geriatric sugar business, continues to prosper according to the classic formula of colonial exploitation — by which a basic raw material or a staple luxury can be cheaply produced for a distant market at a profit, only at the expense of the economy and society, not to mention the entire state of mind, of the producing country.

Jahman, the old Rasta up in the bush, says it's all quite simple. When God created man, he says, he made the black man stupid and the white man smart. And he gave the black man all the most beautiful and naturally provident places to live, and gave the white man all the cold, inhospitable places to live, because if he was so smart he would be able to look after himself. Whereas all the black man had to do was look at a tree and it bore fruit, and if he wanted to flex his brains God gave him ganja in abundance to feed his meditations. While the white man invented benzedrine and seconal and central heating and miraculous tricks with cellophane, and mastered his environment with more and more fantastic technology, none of this the black man ever needed. God in his wisdom, says Jahman, thus favoured the black man and always has. Where it's all gone wrong, it's got to the point where the white man has plundered his own environment and got himself so tied up in knots to maintain his upward and onward mobility that should he stop for a moment — long enough, say, to light up a spliff the size of an ice-cream cone, and consider the scriptural imponderables of those opening verses, about God

breathing life into man, whether before that, man was dead, or alive, or what — the white man, says Jahman, is unable to relax the pace for a moment in case his whole act seizes up and haemorrhages, and he's so egg-bound and ulcerous he's willing to spend $100 a day to see how a barefoot illiterate like him can live for free.

And the trouble is, says Jahman, it's a small island. He can't keep moving to stay one step ahead of the new roads, if they keep on building the hotels. And if they don't and the bauxite companies pull out, the country will go broke.

Jahman, you must understand, is suffering. He's sitting around half-naked in the shade of a swaying palm listening to himself talk, and if he's thirsty he just has to shin up the nearest tree and chop down a fat green coconut, or better still send a boy to do it, and if he's hungry he can just pick something, and if he's feeling fractious, he says, what he likes to do is swim right out to sea as far as he can till he's fighting for air and his arms are like lead and his toes cramp up, and then he sees if he can get back alive. But Jahman doesn't like it here. He's homesick. He's waiting for the Lion of Judah to call him home to Zion.

By the rivers of Babylon,
Where he sat down,
And there he went
When he remembered Zion.
But the wicked carried us away, captivity
Require from us a song,
How can we sing King Alfa song
In a strange land.

Sing it out loud,
Sing a song of freedom sister,
Sing a song of freedom brother,
We gotta sing and shout it,
We gotta talk and shout it,
Shout the song of freedom now.
So that the words of our mouth,
And the meditation of our heart
Be acceptable in thy sight
Over I

B. Dowe and F. McNaughton. Melodians

The Rastafarian Brotherhood first sprang up in Jamaica in the thirties, in the wake of Marcus Garvey. Garvey was a messianic Jamaican evangelist who went around Harlem and the south side of Chicago in the twenties prophesying the coronation of a black king in Africa who would redeem the lost tribes of Judah and call them home. He didn't have a lot of success. His United Negro Improvement Association sounded too much like Sunday school, and his efforts to establish an independent black state in Africa to secure the repatriation of the scattered millions all ended badly. He even floated a shipping line, the Black Star Line, but that flopped too. Eventually the Americans lost patience with this heretic in their midst, flattering the aspirations of the ghetto vote, and they deported him in 1927. But Garvey was a hard man to stop — all the abuse and ridicule and mute incomprehension he came up against only lubricated his convictions and made him more determined. Back in Jamaica, he went on preaching black pride and African redemption. The polo classes took fright and locked him up for contempt. Worse, the black majority were slow to warm to his theme — his enthusiasm for the simple virtues of thrift and honest toil didn't do much for the pride of the bone-lazy unemployed. He died in England in 1940, disappointed but unrepentant.

In Jamaica today, Garvey is a hero of the state, looming like a latter-day Moses in everybody's imagination. Everywhere you go there's a school named after him, or a park, or a new dual-carriageway or a block of flats. He appears on the bank notes, in the spot where the Queen used to be. His career was a long run of flops and fiascos — but Garvey has had his revenge.

It took time and it took proof — it took the first skirmishes with the Mau Mau and the Sharpeville massacre to get it started, but once it sparked, the black rage Garvey was trying to ignite spread like a bushfire in a high wind. Suddenly there was a new map of Africa, and a new breed of vainglorious black colossi shouting back at the whites and chasing them into the sea. In America, half Detroit was in flames and suddenly here were Malcolm X and Stokely Carmichael and Rap Brown with their fists in the air and the Panthers patrolling the ghetto in berets and cartridge belts and scaring the shit out of white America — and everything they were saying was just what Garvey had been saying all along: that the future of the black man lies in his past. He must rediscover his African inheritance and seek his culture and his destiny in the great black continent of his ancestors. 'Look to Africa,' he said, 'when a black king shall be crowned, for the day of deliverance is here.'

When Ras Tafari was crowned Emperor Haile Selassi I in Ethiopia in 1930, the King of Kings, Lord of Lords, the Conquering Lion of the tribes of Judah — when Garvey's followers in Jamaica saw the pictures on the front page of the *Gleaner* they went to their Bibles. To Revelations 5, verses 2, 5 and 6, where it says: 'And I saw a strong Angel proclaiming with a loud voice, "Who is worthy to open the book, and to loose the seals thereof?" . . . And one of the elders sayeth unto me "Weep not: behold, the Lion of the tribe of Judah, the Root of David, hath prevailed to open the book and loose the seven seals thereof. And I beheld, and, lo, in the midst of the throne and of the four beasts, and in the midst of the elders, stood a Lamb as it had been slain, having seven horns and seven eyes, which are the seven spirits of God set forth unto all the earth."' And later, when Ethiopia fell to the Italians, and pictures appeared in the paper of Selassie standing fast on what they said was an unexploded bomb, they went to Revelations 19, verse 19, where it says:

The Government-owned Font Hill property in
St Elizabeth has been taken over by Rasta-
farians, according to Opposition spokesman
William McLaren.

He said some 16 Rastafarians from a section
of Westmoreland had chased the overseer off
the property and taken over his house and office.

'And I saw the beast, and the kings of the earth,
and their armies, gathered together to make war
against him that sat on the horse, and against his
army.' And when Selassie returned triumphant to
Ethiopia in 1941 they went to the next verse: 'And
the beast was taken, and with him the false prophet
that wrought miracles before him, with which he
deceived them that had received the mark of the
beast, and them that worshipped his image. These
both were cast alive into a lake of fire burning with
brimstone.' And it all became clear. They recognized
Selassie as the Lion, the One True God of the prophecy — not God's vicar or His immaculate offspring
but the Living God, Old Alpha himself.

Selassie himself never went so far as to acknow-
ledge his divinity, not in so many words. But the old
gnome was perched on the oldest throne in Africa,
if not the world, the direct descendent of the legendary issue of King Solomon and the Queen of Sheba,
heir to the ancient Ethiopian Empire of all Africa —
and in his prime, before he was overtaken by senility
and mutiny, Selassie spared nothing and nobody in
living up to his legend. He certainly didn't spare his
own people, who died like flies from chronic star-
vation with the Emperor's name on their lips, while
he and his entourage of relatives and libertines spoiled
themselves to death in Addis Ababa.

The Lion had the cunning of a fox — he knew, like
Papa Doc did, that his power derived from imagery
and depended on his celebrity, and his public ap-
pearances were always brilliantly theatrical *tours de
force*.

He kept lions in the Palace, great mangy beasts
prowling round the garden. They say he slept with
them at his feet, and he was canny enough not to
deny it. When a Foreign Minister came to call, he
often let them loose. He'd toy with them, pull their
ears. You can picture him, this tiny ageing gnome,
down on the rug in full battledress shoving his little
head into the lion's mouth, while Selwyn Lloyd or
somebody shifted nervously in his chair and spilt his
Pimm's, trying to think of something to say — as if to

HAILE SELASSIE I
Emperor of Ethiopia

Central St James MP Francis Tulloch has said there were well over 25,000 Rastafarians in Jamaica 'and it is high time we show them the attention they deserve as part of the society.'

'They are part of our society, but we tend to shun them. But as long as we are here and they are here, it is time we have a policy where we let them know that they are part of our society. And the only way they are going to reach Africa is through the same means that some of our older folks get to the USA or Canada.'

Speaking as an attorney, Mr Tulloch said the law did not regard the use of ganja for medical purposes as an offence, and asked 'If smoking ganja is religious to Rastas should we not investigate whether or not there is any possible way to make an exception for them? This, of course, will have to be under the most stringent circumstances.'

make the point that what his own people believed, and a lot of the Rastas believe, was true, that he was indeed divine, mightier by far than the mighty king of the jungle. Vain, even childish, but it certainly had more flair than old LBJ taking a table of journalists and staffers into the men's room, there to reduce them to awe and wonderment at the size of his whopping great Texas trouser snake.

Selassie never acknowledged his divinity. But nor did he deny it. The Rastas in distant Jamaica recognized what they understood to be the political niceties of his diffidence, and worshipped him whether he

liked it or not. They still do, even now he's dead and buried and not yet risen. Long before the Army kicked him out and left him to rot, the old gnome had thrust upon him an unimpeachable divinity in the Rastafarian imagination that ignores the banality of his death, and resides not in his earthly presence but in his image, in The Word, in the single syllable *Jah*. 'Lion!' they shout, and just calling his name resurrects him. '*Jah* lives,' says Bob Marley and what he means is in the beginning was The Word and The Word was *Jah*. In life, the Rastafarians worshipped and adored him with such ferocity that

even he must've gone weak at the knees, when he flew into Kingston on a state visit in the sixties and the brethren turned out in force. They came from all over the island, the Rastas up in the hills walked for a week to get there, and by the time the plane landed and the multitudes caught sight of the Lion painted on the side, they got themselves into such a state that the Emperor refused to get off the plane. He took one look at them, these wild demented creatures, barefoot and half naked, strewn all over the tarmac in various stages of epileptic euphoria, and he went back in. He didn't come out for an hour.

Following upon the Prime Minister's call that all idle lands must be put to use, they said that they cultivated a vegetable garden in New Haven. They were harassed by the police and on March 9 the police visited the vegetable garden and requested that they leave the land.

They told them that they could not leave the land at the present time, because the food was not ready to be reaped and it would spoil. However, the police and the owner came again on March 23 and told them that they would bulldoze the land.

The police again called on them on April 4, tore the fence and allowed animals to get in and devour most of the crops. They promised to return to bulldoze the land.

They said that the police had violated their rights, victimized and intimidated them and they wanted a reasonable time to reap their fruit before coming off the land.

What the Rastas say they want is simple enough. They want to go home. Back to ancestral Africa, where they belong. Back to Zion, before the Rivers of Babylon burst their banks and the earth opens up and the whole godless white civilization goes up in flames, as it surely will, according to prophecy. 1960, Garvey had said, was the date for the launch of the great repatriation, but the Rastas are not disheartened by the delay. They wait, as they have waited all their lives and will probably always wait, up in the scrub and down in the rising stench of the shantytowns of West Kingston, for the Emperor to call them home. That was never likely; now of course it would take a miracle and they know it. But that is immaterial. Ethiopia is a *promise*.

There have been false starts. In 1958 a Rasta called Prince Edward C. Edwards advertised a great convention of the brethren behind the Tivoli Cinema in Kingston Pen. Rastamen from all over the island dropped everything, gave away their last possessions because they wouldn't need them anymore, and came to town expecting to go on board. Down behind the Tivoli, huge stinking piles of old tyres burned day in and day out, the *akete* drums never let up, the Niyamen danced till their legs gave out and still they staggered, and whoever felt the spirit quickening in him like a rabies took the stands and testified till he blacked out and another took his place. It went on for twenty-one days. When it was over, there were no ships at the pier.

Until the ships come in, and they know they won't, they will suffer. They won't starve — nobody starves in Jamaica, it's an island of farmers. Even down in Trench Town you can pick your lunch off a breadfruit tree in somebody's yard and most times he won't mind. Another day he might come after you with a machete, but that's the chance you take. The devout Rastas anyway aspire to a strict Nazarene code of conduct. They don't drink — if it's a hot day and they've got a terrible thirst they might wet their lips with a Red Stripe, they might take a taste of rum here and there when they're feeling low — but they don't drink, and they don't eat meat. They don't beg and they don't steal. They live in random vagrant communities down in shantytown and up in the scrub, trusting in God's grace and the healing powers of the sacramental weed to grant them peace and understanding, that they may be acceptable in His sight.

They don't starve, and they don't go short of ganja, but still they suffer. Suffering is what the Rastafarian solution is all about.

It takes a while to get the hang of it because they spend most of their waking life on the point of vanishing into delirious metaphor, and the weird apocalyptic algebra of Rasta revelation only makes sense when you smoke a pound and a half of ganja a week and abandon all reason. Then it seems simple. The Rastas take it from the Bible that they are the true Jews of the prophecy, buried alive in a hostile and godless white society that couldn't care less about the black man down at the bottom of the heap. They

never wanted to come here and they don't want to stay. So they take no part. They have disenfranchised themselves. They don't vote, they don't pay taxes or contribute in any way, because they renounce their citizenship and recognize no authority but the Emperor, wherever he may be, whenever his resurrection may come. They have defected body and soul from Jamaican society into an outcast astral identity beyond the law.

It's immaterial that Ethiopia is just somewhere over the rainbow. A lot of them don't even know where it is. They'll never live to plant a kiss on the deserts of their ancestors. But that's immaterial too. What Rasta offers is the promise of redemption. And when you're down in the dirt and you feel like you've been down in the dirt for four hundred years and you're worse off than ever, even a vain hope is better than no hope at all. It's a solution. Rasta is not just some half-witted heretic sect selling space in the hereafter. It's an alternative spiritual nationality.

The revelation goes on for days and nights, but there is no Rasta Church. There are the odd backyard cells with an outhouse daubed in Ethiopian red, green and gold, a few big crude maps and diagrams on the fence showing the distribution of the races in the world and a few yellowed snapshots of Selassie. There are transient maildrops for international Ethiopian efforts like the Mystic Masons and the Coptic Church. But there is no priesthood, no clergy, no ceremonial. There isn't even a consensus of belief.

Selassie's death might have been expected to give the game away, but it didn't. It was a sinister business anyway, locking the old gnome up in some derelict soundless room, stripping him of his decorations and leaving him to count the days, powerless without his props, an old Lion with his nails pulled and his teeth filed down and his mane cropped, and who knows if there wasn't some old woman dropping a little odourless, vapourless, Abyssinian strychnine in his water supply that slowly ate his brains

like that, the point of departure here being that your Edward presented Selassie with a sceptre at the coronation, which is true, and that sceptre was the sceptre of the ancient Ethiopian Empire of all Africa the very one, stolen by Imperial Rome, and stolen from Rome by Britain and at last returned to the Lion in recognition of his manifest divinity. In return they say, Selassie sent George V an emblem. And the emblem, when he received it, cut the old King down, he was stricken by a sudden paralysis and all the efforts of the finest medical minds in Babylon could not undo the unfathomable hex, and he died. . . .

This is not widely known. This is actually known only to a few enlightened Rastamen who got it from another Rastaman they met somewhere, and God knows where he got it from. From the Bible, in fact, according to an invisible code — a kind of halluci-natory X-ray which deciphers the subtext and un-ravels the metaphor and reveals whatever suits them hidden beneath the evil blasphemies and lies that every Rastaman knows in his bones are forgeries planted by craven white ecclesiastics in the pay of the Pope in an attempt to confuse the black man and obscure the prophecy. They've all got some personal angle on the prophecy they've cooked up on the strength of a little learning and a lot of days and nights spent sitting around in a backyard some-where working on a pound and a half of ganja and debating the scriptural imponderables, which is the way they spend most of their time. *I head rest with Jah* . . .

Bob Marley is sitting round with Family Man and Carly and the rest of the Wailers in Harry J's re-cording studio in Kingston. They're meant to be making a record here, but it takes a while to get comfortable, and so far all that's happening is Bob Marley and Family Man are hard at work on a spliff the size of an ice-cream cone — bigger, like a huge smouldering turnip — and they're falling all over each other, jabbing each other in the belly, and Marley keeps saying *I head rest with Jah*. This oldtime

away — his son issued a challenge from his pent-house in Geneva, calling for an autopsy, and the Army refused. They won't even tell where he was buried. So most Rastas don't altogether accept the apparent fact of his death, and those that do await his imminent resurrection. If they are fools, they are holy fools, and they can always penetrate another layer of subtle scriptural sub-plot and reinvent the prophecy, not just to satisfy their doubts, because they don't have doubts, but actually to reinforce their revelation.

Consider the Duke of Gloucester. He wandered off into the desert, they say, nibbling grass, where he discovered that he was the reincarnation of Nebu-chadnezzar, the last King of Babylon, whose chosen task it was to abdicate the throne so as later to suc-ceed the reincarnation of Elizabeth I and preside over the utter destruction of Babylon. Something

has-been from the radio station is hanging around the edges, trying to muscle in on the spliff, and he asks Marley if he minds if he watches him do the record. And Marley says no, he doesn't want him standing round *watching* him, and the old Deejay says, well, he didn't mean that, he didn't mean stare at him, and Marley says look here . . .

'It look like you want to find out where I head rest. You goin' round all kind of corner tryin' for smart me to find out where I head rest. But if you want to find out where I head rest, just come and ask me where I head rest. If you want to know where I head rest, I head rest with *Jah*.'

The *burra* drums are the old African voodoo beat, and when they get going up in the hills at night, when they start to get to the marrow and the membrane and the Pocomaniacs feel the spirits quickening in them, they jump and shout and testify till they get so drunk with righteous heaven-sent electricity they froth at the mouth and fall sobbing to the floor. The Pocomaniacs are the last of the Pentecostal voodoo churches with much of a congregation left, and even they put on shows on voodoo night at the swank hotels. The Church of God moved in in the fifties and discouraged spirit possession and talking in tongues, let alone animal sacrifice and dancing in he blood. But people still go to see the obeah woman or a cure, up in the hills. All the billboards saying you don't have to get pregnant and all the assurances in the columns of the *Gleaner* that, No, it's *not* true a woman should have as many kids as she's got vertebrae, they all fail to dispel the fear that birth control is some diabolical conspiracy to wipe out the black race. There's still a residue of weird half-apprehended superstition lurking in the cortex of even the most cocksure and worldly-wise black Jamaican. Even in a man like Michael Manley.

In the last election, when Manley ran against the incumbent Labour Party, he took to the hills in his shirt-sleeves, carrying a long staff — the Rod of Correction, he called it — with which he swore to smite the demons of corruption. The five-acre farmers and the dirt-poor and down-trodden turned out in jubilant assemblies wherever he went, chanting *Joshua! Joshua!*, and Manley held out the Rod and cried, When I look at my people, my heart bleed!' And the people strained to touch the Rod, to feel the almighty power of it, and Manley wept and cried 'It is love!' He was elected by the biggest majority in Jamaican's parliamentary history.

On the roads now and then you see a trail of bright blue dust, and nobody will say what it is or why it's there, or who put it there or where it's leading to, because voodoo is something most black Jamaicans would rather not think about. They'd rather leave it to the old folks fixing up little dolls and sticking them with pins. But they all know that a trail of luminous cobalt dust didn't fall off the back of a truck; somebody's got a hex on, and wherever the trail stops somebody's going to get a terrible headache, stabbing pains; somebody's goat's going to give sour milk. Some Jamaican superstitions, like the country people's talk of mermaids cavorting in the high mountain pools, are strictly benign, strictly Caribbean apparitions. But dancing round the fire and offering up slaughtered chickens and goats to a weird galaxy of Christian saints and martyrs and spirits and serpents from the African bush — the

Petitioner told the court that the marriage went well for a period of three years. His wife then joined a 'clap-hand church'. After this she refused to have any sexual relationship with him. He said that his wife told him that her church told her not to have any sex with him, because he was not a Christian like her. He was a Roman Catholic, and Roman Catholics were not considered Christians by her church.

The police yesterday continued their air-and-land search in Manchester for 45-year-old George Lloyd, who is wanted for questioning in connection with the 'ritual' murder of his 19-month-old son.

The baby was killed at his parents' home in what the police were told was a 'ceremony'. Some of the child's blood was sucked from its body and the body was offered as a 'sacrifice'.

deep, primitive voodoo still practised up in the hills by isolated *cumina* groups — is too savage a reminder of ancestral Africa for most people. They don't like to think of themselves as half-naked savages prone to fits and convulsions and haunted by unseen psychic vampires. They don't believe in *duppys* anymore. They don't believe in them, but word gets round there's a duppy playing up in somebody's house, upsetting the furniture and spilling the milk, and pretty soon the whole town turns up and they're selling ice-creams outside. Just to have a look, just in case, you never know.

A duppy isn't a ghost exactly, but a man's shadow that rises up three days after he's buried and goes on the haunt. A duppy guards the Spanish jar, a huge earthenware jar containing buried treasure, but he can be tempted by the sacrifice of a white cock. Not so the Old Hige. Nothing can stop her when she sheds her skin and goes courting. She comes at night in the shape of a great ball of fire and sucks the blood of her sleeping lovers.

An old reprobate full of white rum and Nutriment standing on the corner with his flies open, bawling his heart out at the passing traffic, attracts no disapproval. No one notices. There is in fact one lunatic asylum in Jamaica, but God knows who's in there, the streets are full of brilliant, lucid madmen. From the start, though, when Howell and Hibbert and the first deranged Masons showed up in Kingston to announce the coronation of the Lion, the Rastas scared people. The polo classes and the brown minority and the conscientious, church-going, black middle classes who were trying to rise above that sort of thing, took notice. Though they never put it into words, there was something in the homesick lamentations of the Rastas that they could recognize, and it made them uneasy. There was logic. It was mad paranoid logic, but it kept reminding them of what they were dedicated to forget. Old L. P. Howell went around selling people pictures of the Emperor for a shilling each and promising them it was their ticket home to Zion. He went to gaol for it. But what alarmed society at large about Howell was the way he was advertising the Rastas' claim to another nationality. In an island of immigrants, that reminded the Syrian in his haberdashery that home wasn't here, it was in Lebanon, and the Chinaman sitting behind his cash-register in his duty-free store that home was in Shanghai or Canton, and the British — especially the British — and the whole brown Caribbean ruling class who habitually look longingly to England for their birthright, that the whole notion of Jamaican nationality was a nonsense.

Howell went further. He retreated with his followers to an abandoned plantation high in the hills called Pinnacle. Up there he ran the first and only Rasta Republic in Jamaica. And he ran it like a private fiefdom. Somewhere along the way, perhaps when they threw him in the madhouse to cool off, it began to dawn on him that there was less to Selassie than met the eye, and as he delved deeper it came to him that Selassie was a usurper.

It was he, Howell, who would loose the seven spirits and split the Seal; he, Howell, was the Living God. The Rastas up at Pinnacle weren't sure what to think. But they were living on his land and they had nowhere else to go, so they took him at his word. Gangungu Maraj, he called himself. His wives called him Gong.

He had thirteen wives, all living up there in the big house, and a heavyweight palace guard and a pack of dogs to patrol his borders and keep the peace among the brethren, who were camped out all over the landscape. Every now and then a gang of them would descend on some helpless five-acre farmer and rob him of his yams and plantain, and if he gave them any *rass* they'd hit from all sides with a gale of maniacal rhetoric that would reduce the poor man to blubber. Howell was growing ganja, not just planting out a little herb, he was in the wholesale business. He had the brethren cultivating whole panoramas of the stuff. It was a cruel twist, and the property-owning middle class couldn't stomach the irony of these mad black vagrants turning the whole plantation over to the weed and terrorizing the peasantry. But Pinnacle was a hard place to get to, and Howell held out for more than ten years against repeated police assaults, which grew more and more bitter until it all peaked in 1954, and the police finally moved in in force and wasted the place. They arrested a couple of hundred people, burned the fields, and scattered the entire community.

What somebody should have foreseen was that the more you make people suffer for their beliefs the more they will be willing to suffer, until the suffering becomes the belief. Every time the police went after the Rastas for ganja they were bruising themselves against a one hundred per cent stalemate and making it worse. The Rastas smoke ganja because the Bible tells them so. They point to Genesis 7 and Revelations 22 where it says, God gave man a little herb to feed his meditations. So there has always been an excuse for the police to run them off their patch and toss them into gaol, whenever society at large was seized by a sudden spasm and demanded results. But the Rastas are oblivious to the law. As far as they are concerned, they are doing God's will every time they light up. And every time the police came after them, they withdrew further into punch-drunk persecution-mania. It didn't help that a lot of gunmen and Too Bad Boys on the run found it easy to stop shaving and start plaiting their locks like rampant spaghetti and pass themselves off as peace-loving brethren. The Rastas gave shelter to fugitives because they were fugitives themselves, but it didn't help.

Howell ended up back in the madhouse, disgraced. And the Pinnacle Rastas came back down the hill into Kingston.

Suddenly, down behind the Tivoli there were thousands of them. All these bloodshot terminal euphorics dancing in the garbage and working themselves up into a frenzy and getting ready to spill out of shantytown and come trooping up the Parade into Victoria Park, and raving about Babylon on a thin wire and redemption in Ethiopia which every school kid knows is 8,000 miles away and dying of rickets. Destitute black vagrants with no stake at all in the fattening GNP and the upward mobility of the new Caribbean, and what's more, they were proud of it. They flaunted it. That made the middle class think twice. They've got a lot to lose. Even a man who runs a gas station has got a cook and a couple of maids. And here were these lunatics making a bizarre public mockery of everything upward and onward they had worked and planned for, threatening the very vitals of their ambition, threatening by their example the whole confident assumption that the future of a small agricultural island lay in the unimpeded exploitation of finite natural resources.

When the Rastas did come staggering up the Parade towards Victoria Park, the police met them head-on. It looked like being a fight to the finish with heavy casualties, but it fell flat. It was four in the morning and they'd been on their feet for three weeks by then, and they were starting to fall down.

They'd forgotten their own names, forgotten where they'd come from, forgotten what in the name of all that's Ethiopian they were doing there. So when the police appeared all revved-up and ready to put down a violent uprising — nothing happened. Both sides milled about in the dark, falling over each other. The police shouted at them to go home and the Rastas shouted back, and it went on like that, everybody shouting and falling down and collapsing into each others arms. It was a farce. But when the middle class opened up the *Gleaner* in the morning and conjured up in their uneasy imaginations this mob of lunatics running through the darkened streets, they were seized by a grim foreboding. Nobody had got his head broken in Victoria Park, one or two shellshocked Rastas fell down and scuffed their knees, but the middle class weren't going to let that lull them into a false sense of security. They'd heard rumours of Rastas sacrificing naked children down in shantytown. Naked children! They didn't have the least idea of what was actually going on down there, but they started putting in alarm systems and intercoms connecting them with the house next door, just in case.

The Coral Gardens massacre clinched it. In 1963 a bunch of Rastas went beserk and attacked a gas station in a little town called Coral Gardens ten miles from Montego Bay. They chopped up the owner and burned it down. Then they went off on a mad binge, tearing round the countryside waving their machetes, very much in the same way the field workers took up sticks and stones against the planters in the 1830s. They stormed a local motel, killed one of the guests, and fled up into the foothills where they attacked an overseer's house. When the police ran them to ground, they fought back. This was it, a real shoot-out, this was the armed uprising the middle class had been expecting all along. Local landowners rushed to the scene, in very much the same way the planters formed a private militia to hunt down Daddy Sharpe and the rest of the rebel slaves in the 1830s. This was it, life or death — duck-

ing from tree to tree with bullets clipping the bark inches from their ears, inching forward through the undergrowth on hands and knees, the air alive with the high whine of ricochet — this was the revolution, and the militia were out there side by side with the police protecting their homes and womenfolk and getting in each other's way. It ended with two dead policemen and three dead Rastas. In the next few days hundreds of Rastas were arrested in raids all over the island.

The Coral Garden incident, in fact, was completely out of character. God knows what got into them over there — it may have been something Claudius Henry the Younger said. Claudius Henry the old man was a back-to-Africa preacher who'd gone to gaol when they found he had a room full of guns — actually one shotgun, dynamite, machetes (sharpened, they said, on both sides), sticks, stones, spears, conch shells full of concrete. Claudius the Younger had come back from America where the rage was catching on and spreading like a bush fire, and he and a cadre of returning Jamaican expatriates and American blacks had tried to recruit the Rastas to doctrinaire guerilla politics. They'd misread the movement, though. The Rastas talk a lot and quote a lot of scripture about peace and brotherhood, and go to great lengths to protest that they're simple peaceloving vegetarians who wouldn't hurt a hair on anybody's head. Which is not to say that every now and then the pressure doesn't get to one of the brethren and fuse his circuits and cause him to forget himself. But most Rastas reject a violent solution to their problems because it simply doesn't apply. Their problems, their poverty and their powerlessness, are already solved for them come redemption day. Until then, they can only wait. They don't have any interest in changing Jamaican society, because they've disowned it. And Babylon will surely soon destroy itself.

Since the Coral Gardens massacre, Rastas have been more of a growing embarrassment than a threat to life and property. But the middle classes are

still scared of them — more than ever. And they do well to be. The Rastas are the conscience of the island, and there's more and more of them.

When they get going, when they really get their teeth into something — like what's the difference between their claim to their ancestral identity and the white Jamaican's claim to his? And what's more, why should a Rastaman lift a finger to participate in a society that thinks he's just some poor dope-fiend with fried spinach for brains? — anything like that, deep and fraught with metaphor, so they can work up some pace, the Rastas make the Ancient Mariner sound like a man of few words. They hit cadenzas of maniacal rhetoric that are so fluid and have such sheer velocity that eventually your earthbound linear systems pack up, your eyes swim, your brains turn to spinach, your tongue feels like a lizard in your mouth, and as they go further and deeper into delirious metaphor, you begin to realize that the real reason the middle classes are scared of the Rastas is, they dread they might discover that these mad mindfuckers are right.

ACKNOWLEDGMENTS

The newspaper extracts throughout the book are taken from the *Jamaican Gleaner* and *Jamaican Daily News*. The lyrics opening sections are reproduced by courtesy of the following: *Johnny Too Bad* (p. 18) and *Rivers of Babylon* (p. 70), Blue Mountain Music Ltd; *Four Hundred Years* (p. 40), Tuff Gong Music (ASCAP, Rondor). The authors wish to thank Tony Bougourd and Brian Blevins.